Fred Baier: Furniture in Studio

Fred Baier

Furniture in Studio

John Houston

Bellew Publishing C**C**

First published in Great Britain in 1990
by Bellew Publishing Company Limited
7 Southampton Place, London WC1A 2DR

This book was funded by the Crafts Council

Designed by Ray Carpenter

British Library Cataloguing in Publication Data
Houston, John, 1935 –
    Furniture in studio: Fred Baier. – (Craft in studio).
    1. English furniture. Baier, Fred
    I. Title II. Series
    749.22

    ISBN 0 947792 46 5

Title page
Drawing: bar-stools for Crafts Council
(photograph on page 33)

Contents

Drawing: constructional detail
(photograph on page 43)

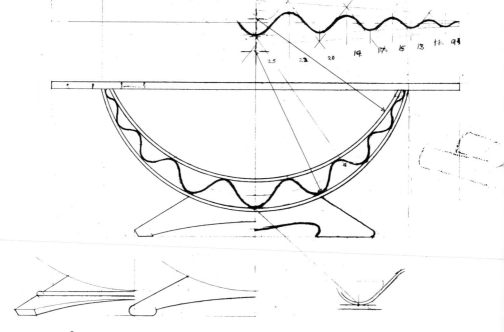

'IS THE SURFACE the heart of things?' A good Modern Movement question: paradoxical, metaphorical and materialist; concerned with truth, its expression through substance and, by implication, its expression in the form of an artefact. The question is Norman Potter's from somewhere in his *What is a Designer,* that compelling manual for the mind, first published in 1969, Fred Baier's first year as a student.

I do not think Baier is a Modernist. Not in Potter's righteously rationalist sense. Yet Baier has made use of several visual languages that say Modern Movement loudly to this unheroic end of the twentieth century. (Although maybe Constructivism and Futurism should be classed as dialect tributaries of Received Modern?) He is (sometimes) devoted to number and geometry as the most honest survivors of older ornamental and symbolic systems. The Modern Movement thought in concrete terms and so does he. The Movement wanted everything to be thought and made NEW – for new times, new needs, new people. Mass-production meant new, now, everywhere. Baier, mostly making one thing at a time, does not make sweeping social claims, but he is no style-hungry Historicist either. His first interest was Invention (as Joshua Reynolds called it): the bringing together of new forms to produce a new result. In the next section he talks about amalgamating things he had seen – that's how he began. There was no thought then of developing original form.

Baier suggests that he began, like many others, by following Pop Art's success. Seeing work by Warhol, Hamilton, Oldenburg and Morris at the Tate Gallery, when he was a student at the end of the 1960s, confirmed the art status of borrowed everyday things. But his borrowings were more ingenious than pin-ups and consumer products. His student work at Birmingham used the human skeleton as a source for design and imagery: a chair – like a pelvis; room-divider based on vertebrae, the ribcage adapted for another piece. Industrial machinery has been a favourite reference ever since the Birmingham days: the college's well-equipped furniture department; the continuing demolition of the city's old manufacturing centre (Baier and two friends were scavenging and selling the debris); and there was Baier's own vacation work for a pattern-maker – a skilled wood-working stage in the casting of heavy machinery. All this fed his appetite for mechanical imagery.

Some of the surviving genres of Pop Art encouraged him to let the things he liked into his art. Pop Art's matey egalitarianism did not attract him – the arched eyebrow (*never* highbrow) comment on consumerist culture was irrelevant to Baier's interest, which was in technological man. Starting with the gentle retrospection inspired by the demolishers 'knocking the hell out of Birmingham', he made furniture in a mechanical mode. Making a table out of bits of a dry-dock, a dockside crane and lifeboat davits comes very close to mid-Victorian kitsch. Ruskin would have taken a very high moral tone about its symbols and illusions. But the table was not an example of 'appropriate ornament' – it is much closer to a tableau of machine stances, a collage of active elements. They are decoratively united: Baier has a keen sense of analogy and employs his dry-dock hinge element as though it was a claw-foot. But the strongest uniting factor is Baier's evident affection for a subject. (They might have been elephants, instead of dockland details.) When the table failed – its essential woodiness twisting and betraying the metal references – he stiffened the structure with hydraulic rams

8

carved in sycamore. Why not? In the playful 'as if' world where wood is anything you want, not even trees are true to their own materials, and a floorboard – freed from function – can be an assertive abstraction.

But a floorboard discovered in what Baier calls his 'working territory' would not remain an abstraction for long. The 'Do Not Bend' labels of historic precedent would be stripped-off and the board (stand-in for Modern Movement decencies) would be exposed to the energies of Baier's imagination. He certainly does not despise the icons of Modernism. Rietveld's Red-Blue chair of 1918 has a fatherly interest in Baier's 1981 chair. This was one of ten chairs commissioned by the Southern Arts Association for an exhibition. *Crafts* No. 50 May/June 1981 assembled a catholic range of opinions, including that of an osteopath. Baier remembers: 'I got really slagged off – about it being ergonomically diabolical.' However, all of the opinions, when packed into a single caption, constituted a vivid response:

A work of perverse genius. Generally derived from the aesthetic experiments of the twenties, Baier's striking chair is unattractive, but visually very satisfying. Ron Lenthall (the technician in the Royal College of Art furniture department) agreed that he had thought of everything. A chair of real character with mystical beauty in the quality of finish and construction. Osteopathically 'terrible'. Freddie Baier is one of the few artist craftsmen to realize the potential of the métier.

'Mystical beauty'! Baier's artefacts command attention by their dynamism. Their structure is an arrangement of parts that are as dedicated to display as a neon sign – indeed the strategies of Constructivism are part of his agile aesthetic responses to every opportunity. But the formal devices of display in this mode have been part of our culture for nearly seventy years. The pioneer Construct-ivists made furniture as manifestoes of belief about symbolic forms and their spatial contexts. Their artefacts were intended to have a vivid clarity as a corres-pondence with the human need for a more direct experience of reality. To achieve this, a whole range of domestic artefacts were deconstructed and rebuilt in terms of urgent and emphatic structures. In 1983 Baier redesigned his 'diabolical' chair,

9

using the same imagery, but altering the proportions, and making the depth of the seat the same as that of the Rietveld Red-Blue chair; like the Rietveld, Baier's chair continues to be made.

Display is an aspect of composition: drawing the observer into the artefact's territory, defining purpose and viewpoints, offering a menu of qualities for slower consideration. Baier is excellent at this slow release of qualities, which is one of the problems of the grander pieces of furniture, or of most other artefacts – including sculpture and architecture. The solution can be found in creating hierarchies – of colour, texture, form, rhythm, scale, for example. The Constructivists had their ways of doing this; most historical 'styles' are founded on formalized practices which are known at the time, or interpreted later, as canons governing their forms. Often academic, but never just a blueprint, these manuals for the mind can be historical espionage for art historians; for makers of artefacts, they are ways to step in and out of the river of time.

Baier's canon-seeking curiosity was probably stirred by his post-Pop Art strategy – 'Design didn't really come into it. It was more a matter of taking something out of its original context and forcing it to be a bit of furniture . . . ' This is the Museum-without-Walls syndrome, spreading throughout our commodity culture since the 1950s. Malraux's exposition of a free-range worldwide traffic in images and ideas undermined distinctive, qualitative conceptions of history and locale. No context . . . not much comment. Baier found his contexts, at first, in the world of work. Mechanistic substructures dovetailed with his own work as a pattern-maker. The last thing he made at the Royal College of Art in 1976 was a chest of drawers made on pattern-making principles – 'You could actually cast it in steel.' It is a weird object, evidently formed by certain constraints, as seemingly compressed and stylistically opaque as an H.C. Westermann. The constraints – basically that all its forms could be moulded and cast – leant some way towards a formative canon.

He acknowledges two other interpretative efforts – the very successful work at St Anne's Court (the Modernist house built by Raymond McGrath in 1934) on which he and Chris Rose collaborated from 1982–6; and the 'Bay City Roller' cabinet of 1983, made during his time as Northern Arts Fellow. The St Anne's project fitted two circular and stylistically emphatic rooms with a quiet and kindly complexity that reappears in Baier's work as the 'Space Invader' cabinet of 1985. The tartan-topped 'Bay City Roller' was a deliberately showy reworking of the Baroque, but in contemporary terms. Lured into the conspicuous by the technical problems of moulding plywood scrolls, he reckons the aim was not achieved: it was too stiff; the format too copy-cat. But forming and moulding has led him on to the successfully Baroque (and contemporary) flow and flutter of technicolor plywood. The Crafts Council's 1985 'Megatron' is Bernini-Baier, with structure as a vivacious diagram of stress.

Fred Baier got all his mechanistic amalgamations out of his system in the 1970s. But the spirit of Industrialism Past still tugs at his heart. 'Dual Quad' is a Transformer (not the electrical, but the Comic mythology kind) which is also a desk, but the writing surface swivels up to cover DQ's eyes – I mean pigeon-holes – and to allow a large abdominal drawer to be used. Made in 1988, DQ is irresistible. But he is a good old-fashioned 1940s robot, Flash Gordon's missing minder, and first cousin to a wood-working machine of my acquaintance. Where does *he* (respect the genre) exist in Baier's work?

Baier must have his own canons of practice and expression. He does not admit to much in those lines, but volunteered narrative, process, structure, as the elements that may shape ideas or, as often, be the source of them. I would add analogy to his list, because he is full of the unifying, figurative, finding-correspondences-sort-of-quality that seems to distinguish him from many other makers of things in this-sort-of-field. I do still see a gypsy characteristic – as though he has gone from one field to another, and in each left a different sort of object, as though he had recognized quite different stuff in each field. I used to think it curiously inconsistent of him not to work in terms of a coherent practice. He chooses not to. But his riskier attempts at invention can lead to qualities of drama, entertainment and great swooping flights of fancy.

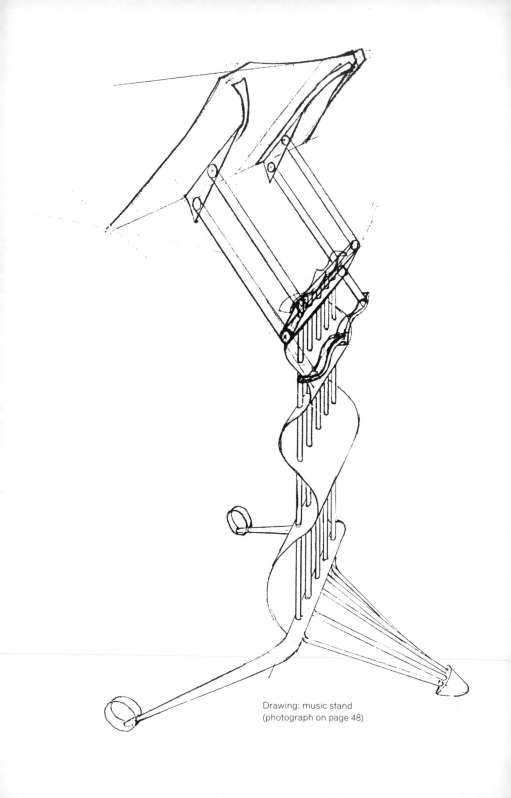

Drawing: music stand
(photograph on page 48)

Fred Baier in his own words introduced by Lucy Strachan

This is an edited version of several hours of conversation reviewing the range of his work. It's introduced by a conversation between Lucy Strachan and me (JH in this text). Lucy is a sculptor, married to Fred, and their second child was expected on the day of the interview. The baby was two days late, Fred was delayed as well . . .

"The piano? Well, that's a classic example of wheel-arches and go-faster stripes"

Fred Baier

LUCY: I didn't really categorize him as a furniture-maker. He's not a romantic at all about work. I'm much more romantic. I think sculpture irritated him in lots of ways. He couldn't get to grips with it. It was too woolly round the edges, whereas design is very definite.

If anything is badly made he says it's sculpture! It's a dig at me as well. But it's fantastic – we're not competing, because we work in a completely different way, and he has an incredible thirst for technology. He's a walking library of how things are made, which is very useful for me. Because I don't use one particular sort of material and he's very useful in providing reference. And he's become much more tolerant of the wishy-washiness of sculpture: even though it worries Fred that it can *be* anything – it *can* be a hole in the floor, because it's as much to do with a mental experience as it is to do with a visual one.

JH: *I'm more familiar with Fred's work from pictures of it, which is very different from the stuff itself, but the pictures portray the work as being many different sorts of design. There seems a gypsy characteristic in Fred – as though he's gone from one field to another, and in each field left a different design as though he'd* found *different* bits *to make it out of.*

LUCY: Yes, he doesn't work to a visual order.

JH: *He's certainly not a traditional craftsman, and he's not a conventional craftsman either in having a sort of practice: a pattern of behaviour which is both technical and emotional – which lets work flow and also provides a visual continuity. But Fred's work makes it look as though he relishes discontinuity.*

LUCY: I don't think so. I think that what drives Fred is what you can do with wood, how far you can push the process – like doing those scrolls (which form the base of the tartan desk). Of course how it looks is very important. The scrolls were very complicated to do, and something that I don't think had been done before. That's what drives Fred: *not* that he thinks, 'Oh, you can do this with wood and I'll make it this shape.' I think he draws it first. But he doesn't draw with technique in mind. He draws freely and *then* thinks 'Is it possible?' There's always a root there from some other visual system: be it mechanical or electrical or computer . . . it's derivative of some kind of technology. He's very keen on it being modern and forward-looking. At the moment he's doing this computer program with Paul McManus who he met while he was at Northern Arts (the Fellowship 1982–3). Fred went round one of the colleges, happened to walk into the computer room and just got chatting and then started playing around on the computers with this guy. And they've formulated a kind of partnership to work out a computer program – although it's based on Fred, it's aimed at industry, with the hope that the whole artefact can be designed on the computer and everything cut on computer-aided machines. They've been working on it, on and off, for

1. Chair 1989 height 89cm
Medium density fibreboard painted with
polyester; design generated and geometry
calculated for manufacture by computer
program developed by Paul McManus,
Rubicon Systems Ltd *Owned by Fred Baier*

about six years. He's designed this chair – the computer punched out reams and reams of numbers, and Fred just made this chair *from* all these numbers. Fred physically cut it up, but the computer had calculated and measured everything. The chair is composed of facets of a wedge: all different sections. I'm sure ergonomics had nothing to do with it.

JH: *So, however eclectic you can say he is, it's an eclecticism that's not primarily visual. He jumps from peak to peak, tumbling into valleys on the way . . .*

LUCY: Yes – see what they think of this!

JH: *Fred has this flair for publicity, for making objects that have memorable and newsworthy characteristics, and for talking about them in a vivid way – in effect, for placing them in relation to his personality. But in all of this, I note that he says he doesn't want to do it full-time!?*

LUCY: Oh but he does! He doesn't make things all the time – he's not chained to his bench and whittling night and day. But he's always done it all the time – he's never done anything else. But he's not obsessive. He likes bed a lot: he loves to stay in bed, loves to sleep; will sit in a chair and just go off to sleep. And those moments, for Fred, are very very important. He says that creative people need a lot more sleep. It's his excuse. We talk about it every morning: 'Just five more minutes' is going to be his epitaph.

JH: *Re-reading this, Lucy wanted something said on the other side of the argument. I chose a bit of an essay Fred wrote several years ago.*

'Those driftings in and out of reality and dreamland are among my most treasured moments . . . My difficulty is with changing state. Whatever it is I'm doing at the time, I hate stopping in order to do something else (unless, of course, I didn't want to start doing it in the first place). I can't bear going to bed early. If other people are up doing things

18

I might miss out on something. Then there's the "Dinner's ready" . . . "OK, just coming" problem. Just coming has been known to take over an hour. But the most important of them all is lying-in in the mornings.'

(Fred arrived and begins to tell his own story.)

Well he wasn't actually my Grandpa: there was my Granny and her two sisters, and all their husbands died; they all lived at our house; one of them had a boyfriend: he was my surrogate Grandad: he used to make things – violas, cabinets, things like that. It was his hobby, making things in his shed. I remember the visits well – I was about nine – he showed me how to sharpen a knife: very important it seemed, probably because I was still not allowed to sharpen knives, I suppose. Then when he died he left me all his tools – I just knackered them in the next couple of years, making tree-houses and bits and pieces. I suppose that got me into it. He was Uncle Bill: Gruncle we called him, because he was a sort of Great Uncle.

My Dad was academic, he taught German, High German. He ran the department at Hull University. He had a little room at the top of the house. I had to knock on the door and I wasn't allowed to touch *anything*. There was just piles and piles of books and papers and it had a particular smell that every now and then I smell and remember going into his study. A sort of *déjà sniff*: as clear as a radio message.

I was always making things: bits and pieces for the house, bits of furniture, crossbows. I learnt to be busy from my mother, and I learnt the idea of always making things rather than getting other people to do it. And after that it was always easier and better done if I did it myself. I'm really just a DIY person – that's about the size of it.

I suppose all the arty stuff came when I went to art college. I was going to do something with design by the time I left school. I was good at woodwork, and I had a full set of tools by then. I knew I was going to do furniture, because I got a job, after school, in a furniture factory, making ships' binnacles, and doing bar-fitting. They did ships' binnacles at one end, and bar-fitting at the other end. I just went there and said, 'I'm going to college to be a furniture designer and I want to get a bit of practice in,'

19

so they showed me what to do with it! That was even before foundation, which I did at Canterbury [1968–9] with the idea of doing furniture, and then I went to Birmingham [1969–72] and did furniture.

And then I worked on the M6 [motorway from Rugby to Carlisle] and then I went to the Royal College of Art [1973–6].

Every holiday I had a job somewhere. I like to be busy – never liked reading books or watching telly – and because it mucks you in with people. All the time college was fine: eight years sounds a long time, but there were all the facilities and people telling you how to do things and stuff: the more of that you can find the better . . .

And then the holidays . . . there was two things I used to do. There was pattern-making: I used to go to this pattern-maker's every holiday, built up a relationship, and proved I was quite good. And I could earn better money than I could in any old labouring job, so I used to go back and back. The other thing I did was shuttering concrete on the M6: that was really good money for the 1970s – £150 a week at the age of twenty or so. You get a drawing and the sheet of plywood and saw them up, someone comes along and puts all the steel up, then you bash up the shuttering round it. I worked on the M6, north of Kendal, for about a year. It was great. When I was a kid we used to hang around there in the summer. Then I got this job. We lived in portacabins at first. What used to happen was that most of the people who work on those sort of jobs are pretty lost souls. Because you go from one empty area of the country to another. Most of them were sending money back home – a lot of Irish blokes, and a lot of English blokes as well. But they were all estranged from their home lives. Because if you worked a Sunday you got treble time, and if you worked a fourth Sunday [in a month] you got six times your usual rate – incentives just to keep the workforce going. But pretty much a pattern of work all day, go to the pub and get absolutely arseholed. No women, nothing.

One night there was this huge ruck between two factions from different portacabins, and the one lot decided in the night to roll the other portacabin down the hill. That was the cut-off point, so me and three lads I got friendly with, we went off and found somewhere to live.

2. 'Pattern-maker' chest of drawers 1976
height 122cm sycamore, stained metallic grey
Owned by Neil and Dul Henderson, Banbury

Pattern-making: you know when they cast things in metal? One of the ways of casting is in sand. You make a pattern and press it into the sand to make a mould and then fill it with the metal. And they used to make the things you pressed into the sand out of wood. Pattern-making is a woodwork-based industry. And I worked for a company that made patterns for the big bits for the car industry: presses and so on. Some of the wooden patterns weighed over a ton.

That was the last thing I made when I was at college: it was my homage to the pattern-making industry. You could actually cast it in steel if you wanted. I even worked out a way of making it in cast components, worked out for shrinkage and all that. That coincides with some sort of statement of intent to do with objects and industry and how things were designed to do a job and not a thought about what they looked like particularly. That was sort of my manifesto of what I intended to do.

JH: *here it is, from 1976:* 'Due to considerable opposition to my first attempts at creating a piece of furniture, I began to kick myself for ever imagining that a design course would be more beneficial to me than a fine art one. Pop Art was the thing of the moment and I was keen to join in. Of course being as green as they come I fell into the same trap that many others did at that time, which was that of sacrificing far too many considerations for the sake of fashion. Design didn't really come into it. It was more a matter of taking something out of its original context and forcing it to be a piece of furniture or whatever. Consequently when the craze wore off we were left with a load of poor-quality unusable rubbish. Still, if nothing else, I learned a thing or two from my mistakes.

There were thousands of things around that people see and use and take for granted, never stopping to look at them and never noticing their beauty. So it is down to the artists to point them out, but if, as in my case, the transformed object is to be used for some specific purpose, a lot more careful manipulating has to be done than in creating a piece of pure sculpture.

Unfortunately we live in a world where, for the sake of convenience,

3. Table 1977 diameter 122cm
Sycamore, stained turquoise
and rust, lacquered
Lotherton Hall, Leeds

everything has to be given a label and you can't believe the hours I spend trying to decide whether I'm an artist or a designer or what the hell I am. Anyway I do know that I enjoy dreaming up and making usable things and hope that by doing so I am developing a closer relationship between design and the finer arts.'

Dock brief

1977, I went home that Christmas, everyone was sitting about watching telly, so I got bored and went off drawing round the docks [Kingston-upon Hull]. It *wasn't* 'What can I make these drawings into?'

23

But the next thing was that I had to make a table for somebody and I used those particular pages in my sketchbook as the reference for that. So the three legs are like the davits for lifeboats, and their feet are something like the rise and-fall things on a floating dock, where the bridge goes up and down with the tide, and the whole business under the table-top is to do with the waist of a crane, where it moves round and the mechanism that moves it is a cog wheel. That was it – I put it in the first exhibition I was in since leaving college: it was at the Royal College of Art.

I went back to see it a week later and the top was all tilted. I had reasoned that three opposing supports wouldn't allow any movement, because the pivot points aren't in the same axis. But for one reason or another it had, because I'd made it somewhere damp and the wood had shrunk: you know all that woody rubbish. I had to think of another component to give it triangulation, so I used pistons. Then I entered it for that competition [the 1978 *Sunday Telegraph* Crafts Awards] and it won. I got an offer for the table, which turned into an order when I said it was already spoken for. Then the order fell through after I'd made the table in less than four weeks. So that was a bit of a drag. But then there was the exhibition of the *Telegraph* Awards and it got blasted in the newspaper and one or two other places and I got the cash for winning the prize, so that paid for doing it, and I gave it to Ann Hartree to sell in her gallery and it was bought by Lotherton Hall, which houses the Leeds Museum's Crafts Collections. A happy ending: pistons, the Royal Family and a Prize. And a night out with the Duke of Kent and the editor of the newspaper. We were in the Savoy Hotel: slap-up this and that – and five minutes after all the entourage had left, someone walked up to me and said, 'On yer bike, John, it's not your sort of gaff here.' I said, 'Oh, I've just won this prize, it's been rather nice and I've been intending to spend the rest of the evening here – me and my friends.' But we were all too scruffy, so we literally got ushered out.

4. 'Star Wars' chair 1978 height 76cm
Sycamore, stained yellow and grey,
lacquered; yellow upholstery
Crafts Council Collection, London

Chair of Office

Anyway, while that hadn't been sold, I thought the reason was that nobody could imagine what sort of chairs to put with it. Then halfway through making that chair the table got sold. So I could still change the chair. Then the Crafts Council gave me the job of making a chair for Victor's office [Victor Margrie, Director of the Crafts Council from its foundation in 1972 to 1984]. I showed him the drawings and he said, 'Well, er' then I showed him the fabric I was going to do it in, which was gold and lapis lazuli in response to the Tutankhamoun exhibition that was going on, and he said: [very, very quietly] 'That's a bit loud for my office,' so I made him a slightly toned-down version in yellow and grey. I finished that first bolder chair and sent it to the Prescote Gallery and it sat there for ages and didn't sell and I thought, 'That's probably because it hasn't got a table to go with it.' So then I did that table there. But actually the original drawings for those two pieces happened when I was in Italy working on the Flash Gordon project.

[Together with Jon Weallens and Terry Jones, Baier was invited by a now vanished manufacturer to develop a range of 1940-ish furniture. It was provisionally titled 'Flash Gordon'. But when the previous year's range of 1930-ish pieces – *not* designed by this team – failed to sell, the project was dropped.]

And that's got a little bit of those Victorian cellar lights as influence. You know, those glass blocks in the pavement used to let light into cellars – and as the lights get broken they gradually get replaced. The technology has changed and the glass is slightly different.

Star Wars street furniture

That was because we'd set ourselves this thing about Flash Gordon, and he had a thing about ray bridges: a bridge that you just went *z-z-z-z-z-z* and it was there, like a sheet of light you could walk across, and the drawings were from trying to make something that would float like that slice of light. Somebody else gave it the 'Star Wars' nickname because they thought the feet looked like retro-rockets, but they're actually those concrete bollards that stop you driving across the pavement.

It's my thoughts amalgamating forms that I've seen: it's not original, not trying to develop original form. I always thought that Pop Art was really nice. I swung with the Pop Art and that's why my things were made in that sort of way.

But it has to be exactly right: anthropomorphic? and ergonomic? There was a chair that I got really slagged off about – about it being ergonomically diabolical. That was really upsetting. So that's why,

5. 'Star Wars' table 1979 length 147cm
Sycamore: plywood top veneered and inlaid
with pre-stained veneer, lacquered
Birmingham Museum and Art Gallery

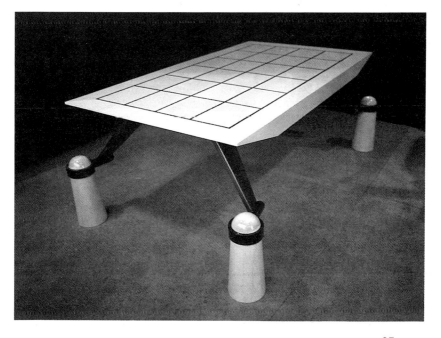

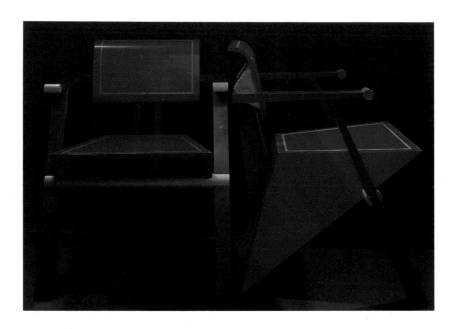

6. Chair 1983 height 55cm
Plywood and sycamore, stained and lacquered
Made by Tim Wells
Lotherton Hall, Leeds

7. Chair 1981 height 55cm
Plywood and sycamore, stained and lacquered
Southern Arts Association

several years later I did *that* one, which was an anthropomorphically correct version of that one. I'd always intended to make the correction, but you rarely get the chance to go through something again. So I used exactly the same chair imagery and just changed the proportions to make it all right.

Turning the Table

The next thing that happened, probably because I was showing these things at Ann Hartree's, was a guy from the Oxford Centre for Management Studies was given the job to find someone to make them a boardroom table. That was the first time someone asked me to make something specific. He'd visited Ann Hartree's gallery a couple of times, seen several people and decided I should be the one. He said I should go and visit their management and show them slides of what I'd done. They thought they were going to get something really weird and wacky, looking like a JCB, which they supposed I'd try and make into a conference table. They came up with the idea of a competition, by invitation, to produce a design. They invited four other people, and kept me involved, presumably to have an excuse to say mine was too wacky. But I won the competition! It was a paper design plus a model from everyone: the judges were the same people plus the architect who designed the building. That was a stroke of luck. And the other bloke, Bill Impey, the one who'd chosen me in the first place, was quite pleased as well. So I got the job.

When I designed it I put a cone in the middle – the table was based on an impeller motor from a jet engine – the cone was chopped off at the top to give a focal point where you could put a bunch of flowers or whatever. And from somewhere down the cone was a sort of circle of spokes that joined in to the table. But they wanted me to get rid of the cone because somebody said it looked like a tit. It *was* bright red, and it had this sort of nipple-thing. So I got rid of that and then the table did the hokey-cokey when you banged on it. That's why the wires are an afterthought. A bit like the pistons on that earlier table: to make the structure work.

It was a good event, in the end, but I didn't make any money out of it:

30

though we did eat well while I was working on it. But somebody said that the only reason that I got the job was because no one else could have made anything so extravagant for the money. I didn't have any overheads, and I couldn't have done it in a workshop with proper expenses to meet. I made it in College at Brighton – Lucy sanded half of that – I had the one-day-a-week job at Brighton, and a guy who taught in the woodwork school had a heart attack. He was normally the only tutor in there for two days a week so they were going to have to close the department for two days a week and stop anybody using it. So I said, if you let me work in there, I could oversee people working there and I wouldn't need money. So that was an agreement. They had a veneering machine and a spindle-moulder and so on. It was warm, they paid for the electricity. It was perfect.

Action Artefacts

We had the most dreadful journey delivering the Oxford table, with me twitching and wincing every time we drove over a bump. And we had lunch at the Angel on the bridge.

Afterwards we had all this left-over 1″ plywood. It's about this time that I made a conscious effort to get away from doing things that looked like bits of machinery. They were to do with the demonstration of adjectives. I did a leaning cupboard – and folding and piercing. I suppose I must have made a few bob out of that table, because I managed to make a few things without having an order for them. After making *Piercing* I was asked to design a desk for the home office (as one of the DIY plans for furniture in *The Woodwork Book*, 1982). My office at home was just this bill-stake: every time I got a bill I just spiked it on. So I made a bill-stake desk and a chair to go with it.

Rewriting the Rules

The next work was this 1930s stuff (for St Anne's Court, the Modernist house built by Raymond McGrath in 1934). I got the job through a chance meeting with Nick Stokes who was working on the house. I got asked to make some drawings and ended up making the bed. That was such a hit

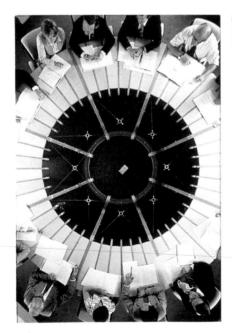

8/9. Board-room table 1980 diameter 3m 81cm
Scandinavian birch-ply veneered with sycamore,
lacquered; stainless steel components
The Oxford Centre for Management Studies

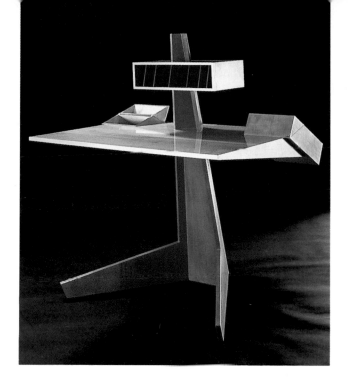

10. 'Bill-stake' desk 1981 height 122cm
Plywood, stained and lacquered
Owned by David Letham, Edinburgh

11. Stool 1981 height 72cm
Stained plywood, neoprene;
upholstered in wet-suit material
Commissioned by the Crafts Council
for the coffee-bar in their new
information area

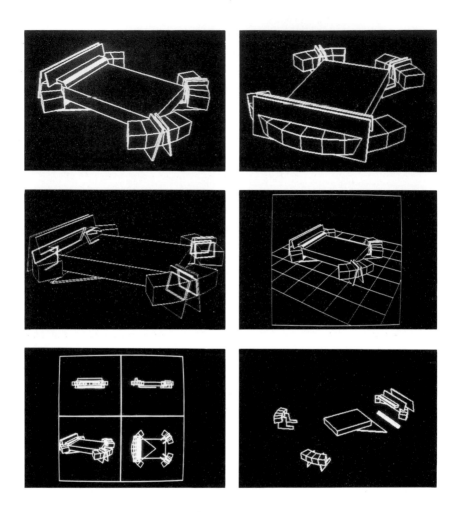

12. Bed for St Anne's Court, Chertsey 1982
Design development via computer imagery using
VAMP (Visualization And Model Programme)
software developed by Paul McManus

that we got *carte blanche* to go through the rest of the house. I say *us* because it looked like it was going to be a big job, and as it was definitely to do with stuff that was 'of a period' I needed somebody to spar with about it. I asked Chris Rose to join in, so all this stuff is both of us, and we asked Tim Wells to help.

We decided we had to find out what the rules were that they worked by in the 1930s. We'd get together and build this set of rules as we discussed the job: 'You can't do that, but you have to do this, because it's fundamental to the house.' Once we'd established that, we started designing. We had agreements about the way geometry should be used, and how transitions worked between a vertical and a horizontal, and also that we *had* to use modern technology. It was an interpretation, but we didn't want to blur the difference between then and now. Our geometry *was* different: *they* had only used perpendiculars, horizontals, circles and squares, but we used intermediate forms and directions as well.

It's because it's a round house that they decided to commission work instead of buying it. Ordinary-shaped furniture doesn't fit into the shapes. So everything there is considered in relation to the geometry of a circle. The base of that is a ring that's then folded up: out of that comes the spokes, which makes the pattern of ovals as they burst through the top. The table-top is a sort of wing shape, both in plan *and* in section: it has a thin and a thick edge.

It was a very happy job – a good relationship with the commissioners. It taught me how to present and argue a case – sometimes strongly against their wishes. I don't find it difficult any more, but I know it can be a problem. If a client has got a forceful way of saying things you have to stand up for yourself and convince them that something is right, and make sure that they are finally happy about it. They were great clients.

We were trying *not* to do pastiches, that was the basic scenario. Looking back it was so much fun that I wanted to do it again. That's where the idea of taking a canon of proportions came from which produced the tartan-top chest of drawers at Newcastle.

13/15. Interiors: St Anne's Court, Chertsey
1982–6 Furniture in burr ash and fiddled
sycamore veneers
In partnership with Chris Rose;
helped by Tim Wells

The Furniture Fellow

I got this Northern Arts Fellowship during 1982–3 and that's where I made the 'Bay City Roller' – that tartan-topped cabinet – as a translation of the Baroque. Everything I do is about narrative and process and structure. The process part of that stemmed from the business of making a mould that would make those scrolls. As far as I knew it had never been done before. Also I wanted to apply a canon of proportions derived from the Baroque. But it wasn't a contemporary enough translation of the meaning of Baroque structure: it was too stiff, for me. You could almost imagine its format being made in seventeen hundred and whatever it was.

But I had set myself a project that was an extreme way of moulding plywood. I also wanted something that was capable of being put into production. There's a process in the woodworking industry of making bent panels. You know the little office chairs that have got a back that's slightly swivelled? They're all made from a piece of bent ply that's upholstered with leatherette. I thought there's loads of companies that bend sheets of plywood and then profile them. It's a really easy process and I thought I would make a chair within it.

So this chair has got just one bend, profiled six different ways and put together. I used that as a format to show off work by six weavers. Which is where I came unstuck in terms of selling them because each of the weavers assumed, like everybody does, that people they've heard about must do awfully well, so when I said to them, 'Weave a piece of cloth and whatever it costs I'll put on the price of the chair' I was being asked a thousand quid for three yards of material. So they were too expensive at first. But eventually all but one of the five was sold.

That's Hilary Auden did the weaving on that one – the first to be sold. It was sold to those people who have that company called Best Products who have those weird buildings with the ends falling down, or with the front entrance jacked up. Those Site buildings. They were my first collectors in the USA. They wanted to buy the 'Bay City Roller' cabinet, but it had already been sold. Then they invited me to go and see them and bought this chair. That was the first time I went to America.

16/17. Desk 1986 length 137cm
Oak and ebony, leather top
Owned by David Blackburn, London

18/19. 'Bay City Roller' cabinet 1983 width
103cm Plywood, laminated, veneered
and inlaid with pre-stained veneers
Owned by Shipley Art Gallery, Tyne and Wear

20. Easy chair 1983 width 103cm
Laminated plywood, stained and lacquered;
upholstery by Larry St Croix;
weaving by Hilary Auden
Owned by Best Products, USA

The Whatnot

I made this Megatron-*étagère*-display-stand in 1985 – to see if I could go further than the moulded plywood work for the Fellowship. This is free-form, done without a mould. Here's how you do it. Imagine a thin piece of plywood made of three sheets of veneer: two go one way – and one goes the other way. You can get it so that the one at the back really wants to stay flat, while the one at the front really wants to bend. It's done by putting a tourniquet between these two points and then winding the string. You line it all up and it just goes like that. It was pretty good fun. It's to do with the idea of the material flowing in the most natural way. The difference between the Baroque and Rococo is that in Baroque you use those flowing elements as part of the structure, but in Rococo it's just tacked on as decoration. So that's that object. It does have quiet moments even though it's a loud object. It was made to put things on but I've never seen anything put on it. If you look at it this way [front on] you've got a golden backdrop, and if you look from the opposite end it's just blueness. From those viewpoints objects put there aren't interfered with. Another element was something to do with birds in flight.

Ruff and Royal

In among the drawings for doing that is the idea of trying to do a ruff out of wood. I've yet to manage that, but I did manage to do this sort of wavy thing for someone who'd won the Duke of Edinburgh's Award. It was those two fabric girls Collier Campbell: and the Duke said, yes you can have £500 or whatever it was to buy anything you like. And they wanted me to make two individually designed tables, one for each of them! At first I didn't know how much the money was – I thought it was the cost of anything you liked, and when I found out I said, 'Well I'm not doing it.' But in the end somebody – I think it was somebody at the Design Council acting for the Duke of Edinburgh, arranged for me to get a lorry-load of free wood from the Crown Estates. Then I made one table for the £500 plus the money I didn't spend on wood. You could say that it was their version – they had lots of ideas that affected it in small ways.

21 Table 1985 length 97cm
English oak, quarter-sawn,
solid and laminated, limed
Owned by Collier Campbell, London

22. Chair 1983 height 55cm and
side table 1986 height 86cm
Plywood, veneered, stained and lacquered
Made by Tim Wells
Owned privately

23. Lamp 1986 height 170cm
Plywood, veneered and laminated,
stained and lacquered
Made by Tim Wells
Owned privately

24/25. Front and back views
Whatnot 1986

26. General view
Whatnot 1986 height 163cm
Veneered plywood, stained
and lacquered;
Crafts Council Collection, London

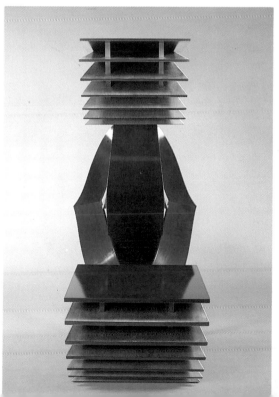

45

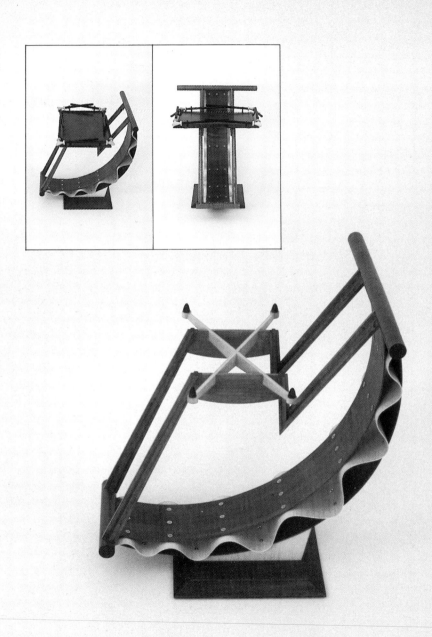

27. Butler's tray 1988 height 81cm
Sycamore: solid, laminated and veneered,
stained and lacquered
Owned by Sarah Nichols

Ruff versions

So for the first time I started to bring on two or three versions of something. When you design something for somebody you go along then you put your foot down and manage to get your way with certain aspects and then you obviously aren't going to get your way. So that's why now I like to do their version up to that point, and then go my way with the other versions. Sometimes it ends up that I prefer their way. But in this case I ended up making three or four different versions. The one for Collier Campbell was limed oak.

Ruff Music

Having worked out this ruff form and made a mould for it, I did a music stand for this virtuoso pianist. I made two identical stands, because there wasn't enough money in the commission – which was for £3,500 – to make one. I won the bet that she would choose the green version, and I sold the pink one for £4,000 to someone in Italy. The first one actually cost £3,500 to make. The sources are pretty obvious: all about sound waves and so on. The vertical rods are the five lines of the music stave, there are details like the little bits of a saxophone, but patinated green, and there's a bracket like the sign you use to join bass and treble clefs together. You can move the support into any position and it will stay there – I had a spring specially designed to take the weight of a two-and-a-half-pound book.

Space Invader cupboard

Mr Knox gave me this book *Bohemian Architecture*, which he had written, to give me an idea of what he liked. It was new and fascinating stuff to me about these little barons trying to outdo each other with fairy castles in the nineteenth century. It led me to wonderful drawings by this great architect – Fischer von Erlach. He used forms of fortification – earthworks and glacis – as decoration, and he designed lots of things with the plan as the prime image, including Mr Knox's favourite building. The idea was a square divided into four squares: then you rotate them out of the big square, on notional pivot-points. I started from there, but I

28/29. Music Stand 1986
maximum height 152cm
Laminated sycamore,
anodized aluminium,
patinated copper-plated steel;
metalwork by Tony Driver
Owned by Suzanna Knox, London

30/31. 'Space Invader' cabinet 1985 height 96cm
Plywood with Italian pre-stained
and burr veneers
Made by Tim Wells
Owned by Brian Knox, London

changed the idea from being a plan, to being a solid heavy weight. The parts above the main form look as though they are pivoting out – and then it started to look like a Space Invader. The central projecting piece came from another of the architect's drawings, showing a key-stone in the middle of a frou-frou window-frame. I met Mr Knox when he was wearing his cricket blazer. It was stripes and piping – so that's where the edging on the cupboard came from – the piping on his blazer. The cupboard has complex geometry: the detailed construction took some working out, so a lot of that detailing is input from Tim Wells, who made it.

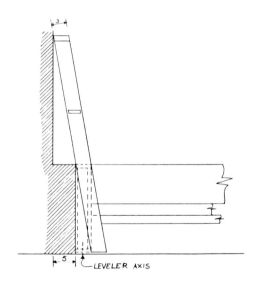

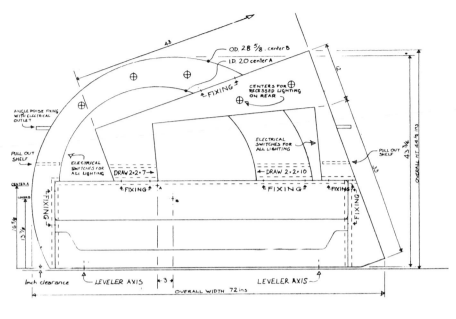

O.D. 28 5/8 . center B

I.D. 20 center A

FIXING

CENTERS FOR
RECESSED LIGHTING
ON REAR

A.B

ANGLE POISE FIXING
WITH ELECTRICAL
OUTLET

ELECTRICAL
SWITCHES FOR
ALL LIGHTING

PULL OUT
SHELF

ELECTRICAL
SWITCHES FOR
ALL LIGHTING

DRAW 2×2×7

DRAW 2×2×10

PULL OUT
SHELF

OVERALL HT. 44 1/2 103

43 3/4

CENTER A

LOWER B

FIXING

FIXING

FIXING

A

FIXING

FIXING

FIXING

16 5/8
13 7/8

Inch clearance

LEVELER AXIS

3

LEVELER AXIS

OVERALL WIDTH 72 ins

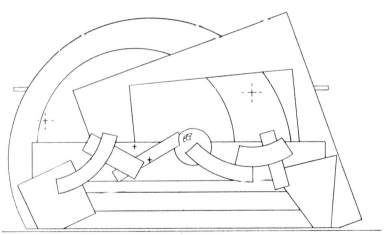

BED FOR ROSLYN MEWS, LONDON N.W.3.
CLIENT :- JANICE & DAVID BLACKBURN
ALL DIMENSIONS IN INCHES
SCALE   0   3   6   9   12   15   18   21   24
DESIGNED AND TO BE MADE IN N.Y.C
BY FRED BAIER & TIM WELLS
REVISED DRAWING FEBRUARY 1988

32. Bed 1988 width 152cm
Maple, solid and veneered,
stained and lacquered
Made by Tim Wells
Owned by Janice and David Blackburn

33. Interlocking table 1989
detail of foot

34. Interlocking tables 1989
length of each 183cm
English oak, quarter-sawn,
stained and limed
with fluorescent colour
Chairs 1990 height 102cm
modified versions by Fred Baier
of: St Stephen's chairs 1987
designed by Martin Ryan
black tubular steel;
printed fabric
designed by Alex Lacey;
sculptured finials
of buildings and animals
associated with owners,
all by Lucy Strachan
Mural painted by Neil McKay
*Owned by Lucy and
David Abel-Smith*

35/36. Interlocking tables 1989

54

The Piano

Well, that's a classic example of wheel-arches and go-faster stripes. That's because of the way we developed the budget on it – and that's because of the bizarre nature of the people who wanted it, Suzy and Eddy Elson. They just love craft. So when I got to their house it was: 'Well could you make a TV stand?' 'Yeah.' 'Could you make a really comfy chair with a footstool?' 'Yeah.' 'I don't suppose you could make a piano, could you?' 'Yeah, I could make a piano.' 'Oh well, we'll have the piano then.' It was as easy as that.

So I said, what budget are you thinking of? They said, well £10,000 is what we thought. And I said, well OK, but then gradually upped the price to nearly double. But when I first bought the piano it was with the intention of making the £10,000-thing, so it's not a virtuoso instrument. [The grand piano is an Ernest Kapps, made in Dresden in 1893, and chosen for its flamboyant interior.] We had a guy who had played with Oscar Peterson who played it on the night it was on show. He was a weird old jazz and blues man with gout in one leg and a stick. He came along and hung his stick on the side of the piano with quite some force – KLUNK! We polished the mark out later! He asked me what make it was, and said, 'Oh no! They're really crap.' But then he played it and said, 'It's the best one of those I've ever played.' That's down to the very good guy I got to do the ivories and so on.

They dropped it on the way in

Tom Wolfe's *Bonfire of the Vanities* has this guy who thinks he's Master of the Universe. He's called Sherman, deals in Money, and lives where they live in New York: above Park Avenue at 59th Street. Very, very chi-chi. I go there, measure it up, measured the lift to make sure the packing-case fits the lift. I turn up to find the guy delivering it – who doesn't speak a word of English, arguing with the head janitor who wouldn't let it in through the ground-floor entrance. It had to go through the tradesman's entrance round the back. We got Mr Elson home from work, and he owns the top two floors of this place. But he couldn't persuade him either. So

37/38. Boudoir grand piano ornament 1988
length 198cm Sycamore, steel, synthetic boards,
gold-leaf; opalescent mica powder and
lacquer applied by Page Lacquer Co;
graphics by Moira Bogue; all added to
piano by Ernest Kapp, Dresden 1893
Owned by Suzy and Eddy Elson

we ended up, three parking tickets later, taking it round the back, where it had to go down a flight of metal stairs with a well where it wouldn't go round the corner. Halfway through this unpacking, the driver, who could only speak Spanish and was so fed up being mucked about and sick of getting parking tickets, decided to lower on his own the main body of the piano down on a rope that should have been replaced five jobs ago. It snapped and the whole thing came careering down the stairs. There was this other guy whose knees would have been smashed to bits on the other packing-case if somebody hadn't noticed and said, 'LOOK OUT!' So he jumped into the packing-case, and luckily set his feet apart so that he straddled the collision as the other bit smashed into the packing-case.

There was a hell of a do. Everybody was suing everybody else. But at the end of the day it meant that the piano-tuner guy got shipped over with his girlfriend, stayed for a week in the other penthouse suite, the finishing guy did the same. And I did the same, and made some more money out of it. So we all ended very nicely.

It was lucky it came down round end first, which distributed the force: if it had been the sharp end it would have been start all over again . . .

40/41. Following page: two views of
'Dual Quad' 1988 height 152cm
Sycamore-veneered birch plywood, stained
and lacquered; graphite, leather, steel;
staining by Custom Panel Co and Spoof
Made by Mike Reed
Owned by 'The Mill', London

39. Boudoir grand piano: ornament 1988

Chronology

Fred Baier

1949   Born Kingston-upon-Hull

Training
1968–9   Canterbury College of Art,
           Foundation
1969–72 Birmingham College of Art, Dip.
           AD furniture
1973–6   Royal College of Art, MA, RCA

Fred works continuously: even before Foundation he was learning furniture practice in a shed which made ships' binnacles and fitted bars. Throughout his time as an art student he had other activities that were wood/furniture-related. For several vacations he made the wooden frames for a motor-industry machinery pattern-maker. With two friends at Birmingham College of Art he ran Empire Workshops selling off the doors, cast-iron columns and other architectural paraphernalia during some of Birmingham's demolition years (1969–72). The next year, 1973, was spent with the M6 motorway team north of Kendal, living in portacabins, shuttering concrete. More pattern-making while at the RCA (1973–6) and since then all gaps in the chronology are likely to have been filled

Awards
1971   Royal Society of Arts Bursary
1976   Crafts Advisory Committee,
          Major award
1978   Midland Arts, Minor award
1978   *Telegraph* Sunday Magazine,
          British Crafts Award
1982–3   Northern Arts Fellowship

Teaching

1979–82 Brighton Polytechnic
1986–8 Wendell Castle School, USA
1989 to
present Royal College of Art

Consultancy work
Design Council
Crafts Council
Ahrends Burton & Koralek,
  architects
Terry Farrell Partnership,
  architects
Mister Luna B.V. Bologna, Italy,
  furniture manufacturers
Practical Styling London,
  retail company
E. G. Records & Management
A & M Records
Oxford Centre for Management
  Studies
David Davies Associates Ltd

Exhibitions

1977 **Furniture Designer Craftsman,**
RCA Gallery, London
Night and Day, Victoria & Albert
Museum, London
1978 **New Faces,** British Crafts Centre,
London
Carousel, Crafts Advisory
Committee, London
Crafts of Elegance, *Telegraph*
Sunday Magazine exhibition at
Somerset House, London
1979 **Furniture into Sculpture,** Ikon
Gallery, Birmingham
1980 **Designer Craftsmen,** Warwick
Arts Trust, London
1981 **Contemporary Chairs,** Southern
Arts, touring exhibition
1982 **The Maker's Eye,** Crafts Council,
London

Making Good, South East Arts,
touring exhibition
Multiples, Prescote Gallery,
Warwick Arts Trust, London
1983 **A Leading Edge,** solo exhibition,
Prescote Gallery at Warwick Arts
Trust, London
The Furniture Fellow, solo
exhibition, Northern Arts touring
exhibition
A Closer Look At Wood, Crafts
Council, touring exhibition
1984 **Furniture, Bookbinding, Clocks,**
Crafts Council, London
1985 **Going for Baroque,** Midland
Group, Nottingham
Five Furniture Pieces, British
Crafts Centre, London
A Collection in the Making,
Crafts Council, London
New Faces, Workbench Gallery,
New York, USA
1986 **British Design,**
COI/Kunstlerhaus, Vienna,
Austria
Crucial, Munich, West Germany
1987 **Wendell Castle School Faculty,**
Dawson Gallery, Rochester,
NY, USA
Plinths and Pedestals, Dawson
Gallery, Rochester, NY, USA
Keeping up with the Jones,
Art and Architecture Gallery,
Baltimore, Md, USA
Summer Exhibition, Snyderman
Gallery, Philadelphia, Pa, USA
New Work, Alexander Milliken
Gallery, New York, NY, USA
**2D/3D, Art & Craft Made and
Designed for the Twentieth
Century,** Laing Art Gallery,
Newcastle-upon-Tyne and
Northern Centre for
Contemporary Art, Sunderland
1990 **Three Ways of Seeing:** Fred Baier,
furniture; Caroline Broadhead,
jewellery; Richard Slee, pottery;
Crafts Council, London and tour

Publications

1978   **Made in Britain Beautifully,** Bevis Hillier, *Telegraph* Sunday Magazine July 1978

1979   **Furniture into Sculpture,** catalogue, Ikon Gallery, Birmingham
Current Furniture, Richard La Trobe-Bateman, *Crafts* No. 41 November/December

1980   **Turning the Tables,** Lesley Adamson, *Guardian* February 23

1981   **Are You Sitting Comfortably?** Stephen Bayley, *Crafts* No. 50 May/June
Take Your Choice of Shelves and Cabinets, *House & Garden* February
Contemporary Chairs Exhibition, Mike Collins, *Practical Woodworking* August

1982   **The Maker's Eye,** catalogue, Crafts Council, London
The Woodwork Book, introduction by John Makepeace, Pan Books
Seeking Support for the Craftsmen, Peta Levi, *Daily Telegraph* March 9

1983   **A Leading Edge,** catalogue, Warwick Arts Trust, London
Crafts in Context, commissioning leaflet, Crafts Council, London
Furniture For Looking At, Sue Bond, *Antique Dealer & Collectors Guide* March
The Furniture Designer Who Revels in Challenges, Peta Levi, *House & Garden* March
A Leading Edge: Designs in Furniture by Fred Baier, Christopher Reid, *Crafts* No. 63 July/August
The Baier/Rose Approach to Designing in Furniture, Nola Anderson, *Craft Australia* 4 Summer
Baier/Rose Furniture Designs, John Redmond, *Design in Australia* November

1984   **Furniture, Bookbinding, Clocks,** catalogue, Crafts Council, London
Playing The Vamp, Pilar Viladas, *Progressive Architecture* May
Handmade in London, Lucia van der Post, *Expression* July
Give More Power to the Designer's Elbow, Peter Dormer, *Guardian* September
The Hall of Inventions, *Ham and High* September
Life in the Round, Amicia de Moubray, *Architect's Journal* September 26

1985   **Going for Baroque,** catalogue, Midland Group, Nottingham
Five Easy Pieces, *Blueprint* February
Five Furniture Pieces, review of exhibition, Jan Cumming, *Arts Review* February
Five Uneasy Pieces, *Designer* March
Art Nouveau and New Wave, Peta Levi, *House & Garden* April
Turning The Tables, Abigail Frost, *Creative Review* August
Across The Pond, Fred Baier, *Crafts* No. 77 November/December

1986   **British Design in Vienna,** catalogue, COI, London
Conversations with Craftsmen, Rod Wales talks to Fred Baier, *Woodworking Crafts Magazine* February/March/April
Designers Unite for Assault on Top Markets, Jennifer Benjamin, *Design* March
Craftspeople Abroad, *Crafts* No. 79 March/April
Parnham, Fred Baier, *Crafts* No. 82 November/December
Baier Necessities, *ID* February
New British Design, John Thackara & Peter Dormer, Thames & Hudson

| 1987 | 2D/3D Art & Craft Made and Designed for the Twentieth Century, Coelfrith Press, Sunderland | *The works illustrated are from private collections and the following:* |

1987 2D/3D Art & Craft Made and
Designed for the Twentieth
Century, Coelfrith Press,
Sunderland
Collecting Contemporary
Furniture, Fenella Rowse, *London
Portrait* March
Street Style, Catherine
McDermott, Design Council,
London

1988 Volume 9 – Since The Second
World War – The Crafts,
Cambridge Guide to the Arts in
Britain, CUP

Collections and Commissions

1976 Parnham Trust, Dorset, *small
turned box*
1977 Victoria & Albert Museum,
London, commission *clock*
1978 Crafts Advisory Committee,
London, commission *chair*
Pinto Wood Collection,
Birmingham Museum & Art
Gallery, *Star Wars Table*
Lotherton Hall, Leeds, *table*
1980 Templeton College, Oxford,
commission *conference table*
1981 Southern Arts, commission *chair*
Crafts Council Gallery, London,
commission *coffee bar stools*
1981–6 Furniture for the Raymond
McGrath House, Chertsey
1982 South East Arts and Practical
Woodworking, commission *table*
Best Products, Richmond, Va,
USA, *chair*
1983 Shipley Art Gallery, Tyne & Wear,
tartan cabinet
1985 Crafts Council, London,
Whatnot/Megatron
1986 Best Products, Richmond, Va,
USA, *table*

*The works illustrated are from
private collections and the following:*

Lucy and David Abel-Smith
Fred Baier
Best Products
Birmingham Museum and Art Gallery
Janice and David Blackburn
Crafts Council
Collier Campbell
Suzy and Eddy Elson
Neil and Dot Henderson
Brian Knox
Suzanna Knox
David Letham
Lotherton Hall
'The Mill'
Sarah Nichols
The Oxford Centre for Management Studies
Tommy Roberts
Shipley Art Gallery
Southern Arts Association

Photographic Credits

*(references are to caption
numbers)*
Fred Baier 2, 3, front cover
Crispin Boyle 33, 34, 35
Simon Bramley 32
Paul Carter 7
David Cripps 1
Ian Dobbie 4, 24, 25, 26
Philip Grey 11, 16, 17, 21, 27,
28, 29, 30, 31, 36, 38
Cheryl Klauss 22, 23, 37
Paul McManus 12
Karen Norquay 13, 14, 15, 18,
19, 39, 40, 41
Keith Pattison 6, 20
photographer unknown 5, 8, 9, 10